T0067474

Based on True Events

APRIL 20, 2013

THOMAS

BEVERLY BRUMBACK

Balboa Press books may be ordered through booksellers or by contacting:

Balboa Press
A Division of Hay House
1663 Liberty Drive
Bloomington, IN 47403
www.balboapress.com
1 (877) 407-4847

Print information available on the last page.

ISBN: 978-1-5043-5518-6 (sc)
ISBN: 978-1-5043-5519-3 (e)

Balboa Press rev. date: 07/11/2016

DEDICATION

Sarah Brumback, my daughter-in-law, who has been with me on this amazing journey from day one. She never doubted for once that I could do this.

Joseph Herron, a very dear friend, who opened the door to the truth for me. He was the first person to refer to me as an author. He was always there if I needed him for encouragement and to listen to my ideas on the story.

Holly Cahall, another dear friend who I could tell my deepest thoughts to and would never laugh at me. She knew exactly what I was thinking. She would give me hugs and tell me "you can do this."

Debbie Klink, my cousin who knew all too well what I was writing about because she was there in the room when the three knots occurred. She helped with the editing and inspired me to continue.

Elizabeth Stanley, my aunt who after my mother's death stepped up to take her place. She loves to read as my mother did. She went over my book and made a few notes for editing. She stated how impressed she was.

INTRODUCTION

"When we love another person, we are on a journey through life with them. However, sometimes death separates us from our partners before the journey is over.

From An Unknown Author

IF I HAD READ THIS quote 10 or more years ago, I would have not paid too much attention to it. But my life is no longer the life that I once knew. Was it all a lie, no it was not. Do I believe everything happens for a reason, yes I do. At times when I am busy living my life, I still will stop, shake my head in disbelief and say, "Wow, this is truly happening." I think back at my life, realizing there were signs that I did miss.

Like the time when my two cousins, Bonnie and Debbie, stayed over at my house one night, when we were 12 years old. There were two upstairs bedrooms with a small hall separating them. That night we decided to play a game, called "Murder", as it was a popular game back then. Blank pieces of paper are cut up, then put into a bowl, with one slip having the letter "M" on it; and whoever had this slip would then try to find the other person and yell "Gotcha." Usually this game is played in a very dark room, although we had the light on in the half bath in order to see the slip we draw with the "M". We then closed the bathroom door with only a small amount of light coming through. We also left the hall light on which did shine under the bedroom door.

As the girls started to approach the bathroom door to draw from the bowl again, we suddenly heard three powerful knocks on the bedroom door that led to the hall. There was a pause between each knock. My cousins and I looked at the bottom of the door, where the light was coming through. We could see what appeared to be someone standing there on the other side of the door. Two black feet stood there, blocking part of the light from the hall. Whatever it was, it stood there for what seemed like an eternity. Suddenly I begin to scream and with my cousins, we ran into the bathroom, slamming the door behind us. All three of us begin to cry and screamed for my parents who were downstairs watching TV. Suddenly we heard the bedroom door forcefully open. It was my father, who was very concerned with the screams.

"Are you all OK?" My father asked, gasping for a breath while rushing into the bathroom where we were hiding.

At first we accused him of trying to scare us by knocking on the door. My father was known for his pranks, and was the main suspect seeing as he knew we were playing a frightening game. Even though the blame easily could have been put on him, he reassured us it was not him. He had been watching TV in the back room with my mother. He said he never stepped foot upstairs until after he heard the screams; and, as badly as we wish it were just a prank, it was not him. Both of my parents just brushed it off as imagination due to the fact that we were really involved with our game, but my cousins and I knew it was not our imaginations. We heard the three knocks and saw the shadow of the two feet from under the door. That night we did not sleep in that bedroom.

I think back and realize there was so much more that I just could not see. I believe everyone is born with a purpose. A purpose to be someone, see something, go somewhere. Every life has a meaning. Was I living two lives with one heart? I knew myself, and just like everyone else would one day find my purpose and my true love. What I was not prepared for or expecting is that I would find it after death.

CHAPTER 1

THE BRIGHT SUN REFLECTING OFF the newly formed leaves on the trees in Iroquois Park gave a photic light effect as Beth and her two dogs, Rico(pit bull) and Minnie, (a long-haired Chihuahua), walked through the park. Dew still covered the leftover leaves from the past winter lying on the ground. Freshness, a new beginning; the start of spring hung in the air. Beth could still see the morning mist in the distance as the sun burned through it. A paved road circled the inside of the park, for the public to drive on; and then another road led up to the top, more commonly known as Look out point." But, for a long time now, a very large section of the park had has been closed to cars, so people could walk with their pets, or just walk, run, and bicycle, not having to worry about traffic coming through.

Beth stopped for a second to give the dogs a drink of water from their bottle, and then she took a drink from her own bottle of water. Beth began to walk toward her car parked in the area next to the horse barn, where people would lease stalls. The people there knew her and the dogs because she always parked there. She felt pretty safe and waved to them all the time. People brought their horses to work with them in the rings to the side of the barn. That morning, Walter and his granddaughter, Grace, brought their horse, Abigail, for a work out. As Beth got into her car, she waved to Steven, who took care of the horses in the barn.

Several moments later, when pulling to their home, she saw Michael, her husband, cutting the side yard. He loved working outside when the weather permitted. Several years ago, they decided to buy the family home from Beth's parents, who had retired to Charleston, South Carolina. Beth had grown up in this home and had a lot of fond memories. She wanted to keep the family home, a Bedford stone ranch with a one-car garage, which Michael claimed as his man cave.

Michael Duncan and Beth Stevenson first met at a fall farmers' market. Michael noticed a woman picking up a cantaloupe and checking the ripeness. Then he watched how she walked slowly over to the next farmer's booth. He noticed her long, dark hair and her olive tone skin. She walked with confidence. At one point, she glanced at Michael and gave him a smile that showed the dimples in her face. He then noticed her beautiful green eyes and arched eyebrows. He knew then, he wanted to spend the rest of his life with this woman.

As Beth let the dogs out of the car, she waved to Michael, just to let him know they were home. The front door led into the living room, lit brightly from the skylight in the ceiling. The kitchen and dining room could also be seen from the living room. The stairs going to the basement separated the living room and the kitchen. And the hall from the dining area; (on the right) led to a full bathroom and three bedrooms.

Beth took the dogs in the kitchen, removed their leashes and fed them. Then she walked to the dining area, slid open the glass door and went out back to begin working in her garden. Her parents had an in-ground pool built a year after they had moved in. But with it being so dark in the back, her father later had a flood-light installed. It wasn't too bright, but enough to see the backyard area. After spending most of the day planting flowers and laying mulch, Beth sat in one of her green glider chairs to marvel over her hard work, while drinking a glass of Riesling' white wine. Looking out across the pool, the landscape was beginning to look like a butterfly that had just come out of its cocoon. Through the years, Michael and Beth had incorporated a lot of landscaping around the pool, two water fountains, cedar trees, bushes and several ornamental grasses.

Beth, a neurodiagnostic technologist at one of the local hospitals in Louisville, Kentucky, loved her work. But her life revolved around her family that she loved very deeply. She was the back -bone of the household. Several years ago, Michael and Beth started a business buying up rental property as an investment. Michael had majored in business at the University of Louisville and he took on the task of managing the business. They had two sons, Nick, now 24 and worked as a veterinarian technologist in Louisville. He just bought his first home not far from his parents. Zach, 22, attended Western Kentucky in Bowling Green. He loved to cook and planned on attending a culinary school. He had been dating his girlfriend, Sara, for about two years now. They are planning a fall wedding this year.

Within that time, Beth and Sara had become very good friends. Both Sara and Zach were coming up to spend some time with family. They loved getting together throughout the months. Normally, the whole family would visit Beth's parents on Folly Beach, South Carolina; but, this summer, with new careers starting, everyone felt it was best to just stay at home. They had made plans for a cook-out that Saturday. In the morning, Michael attended to the paper-work for the business, and then headed to the store to pick up food and supplies. Nick had helped with opening the pool last weekend, and also hanging lights around a tree that was planted in the garden at the end of the pool. When Sara and Zach arrived, they put their luggage in the bedroom, changed clothes, and then went swimming. Nick arrived midday to join them. Beth had prepared the food that morning, so all that had to be done was to throw the hamburgers and chicken on the grill.

That evening after eating and swimming, Michael, Nick, and Zach stood in the garage talking, while Sara and Beth sat in the gliders by the pool. As night fell, the lights came on in the backyard, giving an enchanted aura.

"I'm glad you're sitting back here with me;" Beth said, as she takes a sip of her ice tea.

"I have noticed your uneasiness while sitting here with you. What's wrong, Beth?" Sara asked.

Concerned, she continued, "You always felt the backyard to be so very peaceful. Has something happen?"

Looking straight at Sara, Beth replied, "I have not told this to anyone, not even Michael. I have felt the presence of someone else back here for some time now. I just brushed it off, thinking it was just my imagination. Then six months ago, I began to see a tall, black shadow standing in the backyard by the cedar trees. It appeared to be looking at the back of the house."

"You need to tell Michael," Sara said, trying to convince Beth that Michael needed to know.

"I'm just going to give it some time," Beth replied. Then seeing the concern in Sara's brown eyes, Beth added "I'll tell him." Beth said. She also smiled at Sara to reassure her that it was going to be okay.

Suddenly, a cold breeze began to blow throughout the whole backyard, which made both women feel a little unsettled.

Beth began to stare at the cedar trees, "Did you know that it's said that when the wind blows through the trees and around you, it is the spirits speaking to you."

"Beth, are you okay?" Sara asked, feeling she had disrupted Beth's deep thoughts.

Blinking her eyes, Beth turned to Sara with a smile, "Yes, I'm okay." Neither of the two women spoke about what happened or what was said. They continued their evening of talking and drinking tea.

It was a great weekend but too short for Beth. She had hoped that Sara and Zach could have stayed longer. But they had to get back to work and school, just as everyone else needed to do, a reality check of life.

Beth worked longer hours at the hospital and looked forward to a warm shower and just resting. But that evening Michael had other plans for her. When she emerged from the bathroom, in her gown, she went into the kitchen to get something to drink. In doing so, Beth noticed a blanket on the living room floor with two pillows and a Marvin Gaye CD playing. Beside the cover sat a bottle of warm baby oil, wrapped in a towel, and two wine glasses. Michael came up behind Beth, with his pajama pants and a t- shirt on. In a soft voice, he told her, "You need to just relax and I'm here to help you with that."

A blue bottle of Riesling', Beth's favorite wine, rested in his hands along with a plate of crackers and cheese. Still a little puzzled, Beth gave Michael a smile. He slowly removed her gown and helped her to sit on the blanket. He then poured her a glass of wine. After he had handed it to her, she ran her tongue around the edge of the wine glass, while looking at him.

With a grin, Michael walked over to the lamp, on the table and switched it off. Lighting a candle, he began to remove his clothing. Sitting down on the blanket, hip-to-hip with Beth, he poured himself a glass of wine as well, took a sip and watched Beth continue to enjoy her drink.

A few moments later, Michael puts his glass down, and then took Beth's and sat it next to his. He gently laid her down on the blanket and opened the warm baby oil, putting it on his hands and softly rubbing it on Beth's feet. She slowly closed her eyes in response to his touch. He began to rub the oil on both of her legs. Beth's fingers are gently maneuvered through Michael's thick, black hair while he dripped the warm oil up and down her stomach. Nothing needed to be said between the two of them, their emotions said it all. He leaned down to kiss her breast then her wet, plump, sweet lips. He slowly lies on top of her. They kissed harder and deeper while their bodies begin to embrace more with their intensity. After making love, they held each with Michael whispering into Beth's ear,

"I love you."

"I love you, too, babe." Beth murmured, resting in her husband's arms. That night, both of them got a restful night sleep.

The next morning, while getting ready for work in the full bathroom downstairs, Beth began to hear what sounded as if Michael was putting on boots at the side of their bed and walk down the hall toward the dining area. The bedroom was just above the bathroom, so Beth was able to hear any type of noise in that room.

"What the hell is he doing up so early, it is 5 am," Beth tells herself as she rushes up the stairs to check on Michael.

But to her surprise, he was fast asleep and snoring. Going back downstairs to finish getting ready for work, Beth convinced herself it was just her imagination. At that moment, all that Beth could think about was to finishing getting ready for work.

CHAPTER 2

On a bright summer morning, Michael worked on the front yard while Beth raked and cleaned the backyard. Trying to hurry and get things done, as she intended to relax around the pool the rest of the day. Michael had planned on going over to Nick's house to work on a few projects that the two of them had started days ago. Later that evening, Beth and Michael decided to grill some chicken and vegetables. They had the chicken already marinating in a sauce that her parents had sent from Charleston.

Beth was finishing up the yard work when she decided to walk over to the Canadian Hemlocks and rake out more mulch. As she raked, she noticed lying beneath one of the trees, a long stem crimson rose and next to it was an old, round tattered brass button. She slowly picked up the rose, which had a deep red color, with a velvet like texture. A favorite of hers, Beth inhaled the sweet aroma from the flower pondering how these items came to be there; *someone would have had to lay it here.* It was too perfect still having the morning dew on the petals; *but whom*? As Beth leaned down to retrieve the button, she looked around to see if anyone was watching her, then put the button into her pocket. Suddenly, she felt someone touching the back of her hair. Her response was to grab whoever was touching her; But no one was there. This concerned Beth and many mixed emotions swam through her head. Was she truly convinced that the unusual occurrences surrounding her were still just her imagination or was something trying to communicate with her? *If so, but why?* Beth went into the kitchen to put the rose in a vase and then went and hid the button under her clothes in a drawer.

When Michael came in to grab a cold bottle of water, he noticed the rose. Leaning up against the kitchen counter, he asked,

"Where did the rose come from?" He takes a sip of water. Without thinking, Beth responded with,

"Oh a little girl was going door to door selling them this morning. You were cutting on the side yard. I didn't have the heart to say no."

As soon as the words emerged from her mouth, she could not believe she had just lied to her husband. Feeling guilty, she rushed back outside, telling Michael that she still had a lot to do in the yard. Later that evening, when Beth took the old button back out to look at it closer, a rush of cold air took her totally by surprise as it suddenly went through her body, leaving her breathless. Nothing like that had ever happened to her before. She quickly put the button back under her garments, closed the drawer, and went to take a warm shower.

That night, Beth's lie to her husband and that possibility of any spirit in the backyard, kept her from sleeping. She started to think about the footsteps she heard several weeks ago. The thought of it being in her home was unsettling to her.

Around 3am, Minnie needed to go outside,(Ricco was still asleep on the couch). With Beth, holding the little long-haired Chihuahua in her arms, she decided to go out with Minnie while the dog did her business. Beth stood not far from the steps leading down to the patio, when she noticed something from the corner of her right eye. A tall, slender black silhouette figure came from behind the ornamental grass that stood behind the fountain. She turned to look at this object to confirm that this was not her imagination. She could see what appeared to be approximately a six foot figure, wearing some type of coat, which came to the ankles; and possibly pointed boots. Some type of fabric appeared to be coming off its shoulders and a large brim hat sat on its head.

All Beth could see of the face was a black shadow. This silhouette, possibly of a man, began to move rapidly toward her. Jolting, suddenly, Beth found herself sitting up in the bed, breathing heavily and with her insides shaking. She turned to make sure Michael was still lying next to her in the bed. She slowly lay back down, grabbing her covers up to her chest. She was still shaking inside, wondering was it a dream or did it truly happen. She would not tell anyone what had occurred. It was best to leave it alone for now.

As the weeks passed, Beth kept herself busy with work and the family. She did not want any idle time. She did not want to ponder on the strange occurrences in her life. She had not seen the dark shadow for two weeks now and Beth was beginning to feel some sense of relief. Possibly this spirit had moved on. But the rose, still vivid color and velvety to the touch, was not only lasting but was thriving in the vase.

Minnie started to scratch Beth's shoulder, waking her from a deep sleep as the dog needed to go outside. The little Chihuahua ran ahead of Beth, who was still half asleep, stumbled toward the sliding glass doors to let Minnie out. Unexpectedly, the dog started barking as it got to the glass doors. Beth slowly raised her head, only to find the spirit standing under the Canadian hemlock trees, looking right at the back of the house. She put the left side of her face on the glass door and began to whisper in a trembling voice,

"Please go away, just please go away. I need to let my dog out."

Silence reigned as Minnie stopped barking and the dark shadow was gone. Beth then let her out, which only took a second. She refused to look back out again but she knew if the dog was not barking, the spirit was not there. Again, she experienced another sleepless night. She knew this thing wanted something from her, but what?

One morning, Michael had to leave around 8 am to meet someone at one of the rental properties. Not getting a lot of rest the night before and being off from work, Beth had managed to go into a deep sleep. Suddenly, she was awakened by someone calling her name. She sat up in the bed thinking it was a dream, but she began to smell roses. She knew then it was not a dream, it was the spirit calling out to her. She could no longer keep these strange occurrences that were happening from Michael, and she planned on telling him that night.

That evening while both Michael and Beth sat in the garage listening to Motown music on the radio, she began to tell him what had been going on in the past few months.

"There is something I need to tell you, Michael, and I don't know where to begin." Beth, started to tremble, and grabs her husband's hand for comfort.

With Michael's look of concern, Beth continued, "I have been seeing a black silhouette of a man in the backyard. It appears he is looking at the back of the house. I even had a dream, about him coming from behind the ornamental grass and coming up to me. When I woke up, I was shaking and breathing heavily. This has been going on for several weeks now. I'm afraid, Michael."

At first Michael felt it was just in her head, but as Beth continued with her story, he could tell that the fear in her voice was real. *Could her story be true,* Michael thought.

"Beth, why didn't you tell me about this? We can face this together," Michael said. But thoughts ran through his head, as her husband, how was he to protect her from the unknown? Both continued to talk on how to approach this situation throughout the night. While trying to sleep, Michael held Beth tightly, hoping to give her some peace of mind.

Days and nights passed without any episodes occurring. Both Michael and Beth began to feel more at ease. Then one night, Minnie needed to go outside. When Beth began to go down the dark hall, she shivered from the chill. It was so cold she could see her breath in front of her. As she continued down the hall, she heard Ricco jumping from the living room couch, which is where he normally slept. When Ricco and Minnie reached the dining area, they began to bark at something in the corner of the room. Recognizing the barking as a warning, Beth began to tremble and started to pray that the spirit was not in her house. Both dogs stood in the arch way of the living room area. She makes it to the dining room table, afraid to look at what the dogs were barking at to her right. Beth's breathing became heavier. Her head turned slowly to the right to look at the corner of the dining area next to the sliding glass doors and with the light from the back yard, she could see a tall black silhouette figure, the same as in her dream. Beth's worse fear had come true; this spirit was now in her home.

"This can't be happening! I must be dreaming!" Beth, said, though she could not take her eyes off this figure.

She keeps staring as the spirit begins to slowing walk toward her. It turns and looks down at the dogs;(which are still barking),and suddenly there is silence. The dogs sit down as if they were commanded to do so.

"It is time, Beth, "The spirit said, in a soft but assertive voice, as it walked closer to her. Realizing that this was really happening, Beth became limp and began to fall to the floor. Swooping over, the black figure caught her in its arms and securely held her.

Michael opened the bedroom door after hearing all the noise, and there at the end of the hall, he saw a black figure holding his wife.

"Please, please don't hurt her. What is it you want?" Michael asked, as he pleads to the spirit.

The black figure reassured Michael, "She will be safe and she will be returned." Without warning, both

Beth and the spirit vanished. Michael fell to his knees in total disbelief.

CHAPTER 3

White linen curtains danced out into the room from the salty breeze flowing through the bedroom window. Waves crashed onto the beach and the rocks. There were seagulls screaming in the sky. The echo of people talking and laughing who had gathered on the beach for a day of relaxation reverberated inside. Suddenly, Beth opened her eyes, sat straight up in the bed and prayed this was just another dream. She looked over to her left side, hoping she would find Michael lying next to her, but he was not. Instead, she found herself in an old English, four-poster, canopy bed. The bed was draped with white linen and lace, which continued to flow over the sides and enveloped the whole bed. This was not a dream, this was really happening; she began to shake and cry. With the ability to see through the linen, Beth slowly raised up to see if anyone was in the room. Realizing she was alone, Beth cautiously pulled back the soft fabric to continue her assessment of the surroundings. What she found caused her to take a deep breath; she was no longer in her home.

Beth was then drawn to a large bedroom window, which was to the right corner in the front of the room. She rose from the bed to walk over and peer out. To her amazement, an inner peace swept through her as she took in the ocean and its surroundings. Like a frame, the window held the most beautiful picture that she had ever seen. A cedar tree shaded the side of the house; with bushes and flowers in the front. Further along, was the vibrant color of a pink beach, with large black rocks projecting from the sand, and a crystal clear ocean crashing upon them. She saw people playing and lying on the beach. Suddenly, Beth emerged from the spell that was cast on her from the breath taken scenery. Backing away from the window, she noticed on the table a plate with a metal cover over it. Beth lifted it to find oatmeal and whole wheat toast prepared possibly for her, but she was too overwhelmed from the occurring events to think of food. Also lying on the table was a small, pocket purse with a long shoulder strap. Next to it was some type of paper currency. She then turned to look closely at the bedroom where she stood. Large sand-colored tile covered the floors and a salmon hue graced the walls. There was white trim from the ceiling to the floor and in the corner, to the right side of the bed, sat a large, tan wingback chair with a small table to the left side. A small round table with two chairs sat under the window. Across from the right side of the bed; was a bathroom. There on the floor was sand-colored marble.

Beth walked to the bathroom and looked it over. Large, light brown tile covered the walls and the shower area. Coral accessories sat about. Beth found all her needs in toiletries. She shuffled back into the bedroom and opened the closet, only to find batik dresses; (of many different colors), shoes, straw hats, and undergarments.

"Is this a dream? It is all so surreal." Beth rubbed her face, as she continued looking in the bedroom. She knew she needed to find help. As if in a fog, she extracted one of the dresses and a pair of shoes from the closet and lumbered back to the bathroom. She cleaned up, put on the dress and slipped on a pair of shoes.

Quickly walking back into the bedroom, and over to the table, she picked up the paper currency, placed it in the purse, and strung the purse strap around her neck. Creeping to the door, she slowly opened it and looked to make sure that no one was there. Then she scurried down the staircase to the front door. Beth opened the door a few inches, only to find what she saw from the bedroom window, serenity and beauty.

With the ocean breeze blowing through her hair and dress, she closed her eyes for a second as she raised her head toward the warm sun; an inner calmness came over her. Several little rings from a moped going down the street interrupted her serenity. She opened her eyes, and then tiptoed onto a short narrow cobblestone path that lead to the street. Across from the cottage she had just left, a path appeared to lead down to a beach. There she saw several adults and children enjoying themselves on the beautiful pink sand. It was not a very large area. Amazed at the calm she felt, Beth considered that the spirit might somehow have something to do with her feeling this way. But she had to find out where she was and try to get help. Beth walked up to a woman who sat under a large umbrella, reading a book.

"I'm sorry to brother you. But I came in very late last night and had a few drinks. Could you tell me what beach this is?" Beth asked, as she waited patiently for the woman's answer. The woman then turned to Beth, as she removed her sunglasses and looked up at her. "Sure, this is Tobacco Bay, you're in Bermuda." As Beth tried to stay composed, she replied with a forced smile, "Oh yes, that's right." The woman continued, "King's Square is only a 15 to 20 minute walk, but it is all up hill. There is a lot to see there, several shops and restaurants. I think you would really like it."

"Oh, thank you so very much," Beth said. She watched the woman pointing the way to King's Square. Beth decided to take the woman's advice and go to King's Square. She was sure that she would be able to get help there.

Once Beth entered King's Square, she saw several shops and restaurants. There was a waterfront. Where several small boats and large yachts were docked in the harbor. Not far on another street there were Federal-style buildings, painted in pale yellow, pink, blue, and red colors. The streets had the same small path from the cottages, made of cobblestone with a number of historic sites within walking distance. Several people walked the streets, going in and out of shops that lined the area. People were drinking their morning coffee on the sidewalks at the small cafes'. She knew they must be a mix of locals and tourists. Beth felt that possibly she could get help from the police. What else was she to do other than to talk to them, but how to find them was the question. She decided to enter one of the shops, pretending to be a tourist. She walked straight from the sidewalk into a quaint and unique room, full of merchandise that could not be found in the states. The items sat on glass shelves and behind those shelves were walls of mirrors, which lined one side of the store. Delightfully old, pastel colors of yellow and blue adorned the other walls. From the front of the store (which had silk scarves, t-shirts, towels and designer handbags), you could continue to two other rooms leading to the back, which had several beautiful antiques.

While looking at some cedar items, Beth had a sales person approach her asking,

"Can I help you with anything?"

"I really like this picture frame. Is it made from cedar?" Beth said, while hoping that this person could lead her to the police station.

"Yes, it is cedar," the young sales person said with a British accent.

"I'd like to purchase it, please;" Beth said, as she walked up with the sales lady. "Oh, and by the way, where is the police station located?" She asked rather matter-of factly. And as the sales lady looked up at her, she continued in a calm voice, "Just in case I get lost."

"You can go up a few blocks and on your right is Duke of York Street. The station's street number is 22. I hope you enjoy your stay." She said with a smile, handing Beth the neatly wrapped package.

Once leaving the shop, she headed to Duke of York Street. Once there, she found the police station, a square two-story white building that had two steps leading up to the front doors. She stopped at the bottom step and began to think how they would react to her story of an spirit kidnapping her and bringing her to Bermuda. But what else was she to do? Suddenly, she realized she had no identification to prove who she really was. As Beth stood there, she felt someone touching her arm. She saw what appeared to be an older Bermudian gentleman; wearing white Bermuda shorts and a floral shirt.

"Miss,miss, my name is Samuel, my granddaughter…." he said with a British accent, pointed behind him at the girl standing there. "Her name is Theresa, and she is selling a few products that her grandmother helped her make. The best Bermuda rum cake on the whole island made from Black Seal Rum. She also has some jellies made with sherry. Most of the jellies were sold earlier though."

"I'm sorry, sir, but......" Beth said, trying to continue up the two steps.

"How about if we gave you just a small sample of the cake?" Samuel said, as he became more persistent.

"No. Thank you," Beth said, as she put her foot on the next step.

Suddenly, she felt a tight grip on her arm and turned to see that Samuel now had a hold of her.

"You don't want to do this, Miss," Samuel said, in a pleading voice.

She stepped back down on the sidewalk where Samuel stood and looked straight at him.

"And why shouldn't I?" Beth asked, puzzled as to whom this stranger was, and what he was up to.

Samuel, then turns to his granddaughter, "Sweetheart, would you mind going over there and waiting for your grandfather."

As Theresa walked over to one of the black metal benches in front of a shop, Samuel turned to Beth and asked her to sit over in an area away from the public. At first, Beth was a little concerned about going with this man off Duke of York Street. But for some reason, she went anyway.

"You never answered my question, why shouldn't I go to the police station? You do not know me, sir, and the situation that I am now in," Beth said, as she is faced Samuel, sitting on a metal bench and still afraid of whom this person was. She then hears a voice coming from behind her.

"Samuel, I think you need to help Theresa with her cakes and jellies. I'll sit here and keep your friend company." The voice came from an unknown woman, who suddenly appeared from nowhere. This woman appeared to be very confident with herself. A small frame lady, she wore a pastel patchwork muumuu, a straw hat, with a straw tote over her shoulder with low-wedge sandals. She took Samuel's place on the bench, next to Beth.

"It was nice talking to you. Have a good day, Miss. I'm sure we will meet again," Samuel said, as he left to catch up with his granddaughter. The woman introduced herself as Tara Teresa Wilkerson, but the people who know me call me TT, I am Samuel's wife and Theresa's grandmother.

"Do you know me?" Beth asked with uncertainty.

"Yes, I do," said TT, she had a warm smile and her almond shaped dark brown eyes, which gave Beth little comfort.

"But how?" asked Beth, being more than a little puzzled.

"I know who brought you here, his name is Thomas," said TT, as she watched tears beginning to flow from Beth's eyes. Beth was afraid and confused. As TT reached for Beth's hand, to comfort her, she told her, "You are safe with Thomas; he has been with you for a very long time, he has been your protector."

"I don't understand any of this, why me?" Beth asked, her lips trembling.

"Child, things happen that we cannot explain 'til later and this is one of those times. You need to go back to the cottage. But remember, you are safe," said TT, as she pulled out a handkerchief to hand to Beth.

Still crying, Beth told her, with pleading eyes, "All I want to do is go home."

TT replied, "That is not an option, I need to go now, I'm a very busy lady."

As TT rose and began to walk away, Beth asked her, "So I'm just left alone on this island?"

TT turned to reply, "Oh no, child, you are never alone. We are all not far from you and watching over you, including Thomas. Just call to us and someone will be there."

As TT continued down the street, Beth remained seated on the metal bench trying to process what had just happened and decide what she should do next.

Feeling exhausted and worn down, Beth felt she did not have a choice other than to do what TT said, go back to the cottage. As she began to meander toward the street that brought her into the town, she heard what sounded like a small motor vehicle behind her. She stopped to let it pass. It did not, instead it pulled up next to her, causing her to fear for her safety.

"Miss, let me take you back to the cottage." It was Samuel, on his scooter. He wanted to make sure she got back safely. Somewhat relieved once she saw who it was, Beth felt this stranger, who she had only met a few minutes earlier, was a gentle soul. Beth stood looking at him, and then climbed on the back of the scooter. To secure her position, she put her arms around his waist, and then they puttered on down the road. Samuel pulled up in front of the small two-story white cottage. Beth then climbed off the scooter, facing the cottage.

She turned back to Samuel with tears in her eyes, asking, "What am I to do now?"

"You will be guided. Do not be fearful of Thomas, he is a very strong spirit. You will be protected," Samuel said, as he began to pull away and head down the street.

Beth creeped up the short-cobblestone path leading to the front door. With each step, she inhaled the fragrance of the flowering bushes and plants, which lined the front and sides of the cottage. She then found herself at the front red door. She paused then, slowing turning the knob to let herself in. Beth entered the cottage, closing the door behind her with her hands still on the knob, wanting to turn and run back out. She stood there for a minute more then remembered what Samuel told her, "That I would be guided." She then knew the next move was not her's but that she was to wait for Thomas to make it.

CHAPTER 4

ST GEORGE, BERMUDA: AS BETH releases the door knob from inside; she let out a sigh, and then began to walk farther into the living quarters of the cottage on the first floor. She stood there taking it all in for a moment. The oak stairs, which she had run down that morning, were to her left, about four feet from the front door. Sea-foam walls, trimmed in oak, met her eyes. A beige couch of a pale floral design sat to the right of the room, flanked each side by two oak end tables. Across from the sofa, was a brick fireplace with a pink marble hearth. A beige wing-back chair sat to the left, in the corner. On the other side of the chair, white linen curtains flowed from an open window, trimmed in black and facing the front of the cottage. The combination of sweet aroma, from the flowers in the small gardens surrounding the cottage, along with the refreshing smell of the salty ocean breeze pleasured Beth's sinuses and brought needed tranquility. The anxiety she had felt, when first entering the cottage, had vanished, replaced instead by a strong energy that filled the room.

Beth had felt this energy before back at her home, in Kentucky, and now here in Bermuda, as she cautiously moved through the downstairs, she saw an archway leading into the kitchen. She found a side window identical to the one in the living room with a small oak table and two chairs sitting under it. In the center of the table stood a long stem crimson rose. *Could this rose have been from him, the spirit?* Beth asks herself. In the galley kitchen, the cabinets were white with black knobs along with a black granite counter top. The appliances were a black color along with the sink, which had a window above it looking out to the back yard. With Beth now being more relaxed, she was hungry. Figuring the food she had left upstairs that morning was spoiled now, she hoped that there might be food in the refrigerator. In opening the refrigerator, Beth did find a plate of cut-up fruit, crackers, and a piece of rum cake with a bottle of water to the side. She brought her findings to the table, sat down and began to eat while looking out the side window. Still very saddened over the occurrences in the past 10 hours, she wondered what this spirit's next move would be.

While Beth finished eating, she noticed three children walking up to the front of the cottage. Suddenly, there was a knock at the door. She walked up to the front window and carefully looked out to check on who it could be. It was

Theresa, TT and Samuel's granddaughter, and three of what appeared to be her friends. Wondering what this could be about, she slowly opened the door.

"I hope we didn't startle you, but my Nana sent me to make sure you were okay," Theresa said, looking up at Beth and waiting for a response.

"She doesn't look like she is crying to me," said a younger boy.

Theresa quietly turned to him with her finger pressed to her lips, "Shh, Rodi," she said. Then she turned back to Beth, telling her, "This is my nine year old brother. He just tagged along with us. And these are my two best friends Erica and Nori. We are eleven and go to the school together."

"Hi, Rodi,Erica and Nori," Beth said with a slight smile. Then she told them all, "Thank you for stopping by, but I'm okay. I just finished eating some food that was left in the refrigerator."

"Well, that was nice of him," Theresa said, whose comment was very blunt, and took Beth by surprise with her statement.

"And who are you referring to?" Beth asked.

"Thomas, of course," Theresa said, with a snapping voice.

Beth felt that this child knew this spirit and possibly knew him well. She wanted to pursue the matter further, but was exhausted from today's ordeal. She was still trying to deal with this situation that she was in. Beth hoped to have another opportunity to talk to Theresa, but for now she just wanted to take a shower and sleep. So she told the children that she was fine and was going to lie down. As they left, Beth closed the door and started up the stairs. After her shower, Beth had noticed that she grew sleepier and could only think of going to bed under the large canopy. A strong energy was still present. Was this spirit making Beth feel tired and if so why? As she laid her head down on the pillow and pulled the covers over her shoulders, she fell fast asleep.

Louisville,Kentucky: Michael was still in disbelief over what he had just witnessed….. a black spirit holding his wife and then just vanishing with her. He was able to find the strength to pull up from the floor and sit at the dining room table with his head in his hands crying. He couldn't even think straight. How in the name of God, can anyone believe this story when he can't even grasp it himself? He felt as if all his strength had been drained from his body. He pushed himself from the dining room table. Michael shuffled toward the bedroom. He was barely able to get back to bed before he was sound asleep. Later that night, the dark spirit stood in the corner of Beth and Michael's bedroom, watching Michael; the dark shadow creeped over to the side of the bed as if he were checking on him. In a whispering voice, the spirit said, "I am sorry." With that, the entity stepped back from the bed and vanished.

St. George,Bermuda: After checking on Michael, Thomas appeared in front of the four- posted bed where

Beth slept. He sneaked to the left side of the bed and pulled back the white linen to check on her. Thomas stood there for just a moment looking at her, and then released the canopy, letting it fall back into place. He then drifted over to the wing-back. He removed his duster and hat, laying them across the chair, and then sat down and laid his head back as if he were resting.

Louisville,Kentucky: The next morning, Michael opened his eyes, asking himself if it was just a dream. He quickly touched Beth's side of the bed only to realize she was still gone. He sat up on the side while running his fingers through his thick black hair. He then walked over to the bedroom window hoping he would find Beth in the yard working, thinking that he was losing his damn mind. Michael went to the bathroom, sat on the toilet, and then looked into the mirror wondering what he was supposed to do. Finally he forced himself to move down the hall and into the kitchen, wondering if he should call someone. *What proof do I have, none.* He poured a glass of Coke to try to wake up, then went out to the garage (his man cave), and sat down to gather his thoughts. He tried to remember what happened last night after Beth vanished with the spirit. *Is it my imagination or was this thing in the room last night*? As Michael began to shake with fear and uncertainty, a strong gust of wind began blowing outside. Drawn to go out to the backyard, Michael walked out as the wind began to swirl around him.

As he watched the leaves on the trees turning upside down, showing their silver lining, he remembered what Beth once said, "When the wind blows, it is the spirits speaking to you."

Michael had never been much of a believer in this type of nonsense but this morning, he felt different. He knew something, or someone, was trying to connect to him. Michael could feel the energy.

"I know you are here and you were here last night also," Michael found the courage to say. "Is Beth okay, please let me know,"

Without warning, Michael heard a whispering voice. "She is safe, and no harm will come to her. I promise you this." He knew this had to be the spirit that took Beth. Instantly, there was silence, the wind had stopped. Michael sat at the patio table looking down. "I'm praying for your safe return, Beth. I love you so very much and can't imagine going on without you."

CHAPTER 5

St. George,Bermuda: Several knocks at the door, awoke Beth. Still half asleep, she ran down the stairs. Hoping it was Michael coming to take her home, instead, she found Theresa and her friends again, asking her to have breakfast at her grandmother's house. Beth closed her eyes, covering her face with her hands in disappointment that it was not Michael, and in an attempt to hide her tears.

"My Nana said that I was not to take a 'no' for an answer. So what is your answer?" Theresa asked. Ready to escort Beth to TT's home, she looked straight into Beth's eyes and waited.

"It appears I don't have much of a choice, do I? Beth asked, as she removed her hands from her face to answer Theresa's question. With a somber voice, Beth added, "Okay, but I need to get ready first."

With a big smile, Theresa and her friends waited outside. When Beth went back upstairs, hearing the girls shrill giggles, she looked out the window and saw them playing jump rope while waiting for her.

A half hour later, Beth emerged from the cottage, wearing a bright yellow and blue sundress with black sandals. The children ran up to her and with Theresa taking Beth's hand, together they walked to TT and Samuel's home for breakfast. The walk was a little bit uphill, but it soon flattened out. They strolled past cottages along the way. Concrete walls, with flowering plants cascading over them, lined these cottages; a bright blue sky shone above, with just a few clouds. Seagulls flew overhead, with their screams echoing. People zipped by on scooters and they passed others walking. It was a very peaceful walk other than Theresa and her friends talking and asking Beth questions, which did not really bother her.

She was taken back with the beauty of the island: enchanting turquoise waters surrounding the black, volcanic rocks. There were also exquisite-looking pink sand beaches with a combination of coral. Beth could see colorful houses dotting the Bermuda hills. It appeared that a giant treasure chest filled with colored pastel gem stones that had been spilled over this island, glistening in the sun. There were scads of historic sites and, of course, the warm friendly people of Bermuda that they met on the way to TT and Samuel's home. As they turned on the road to reach the home, Beth noticed a few cows crossing in front of them.

She thought how strange it was to see cows on such an exotic island.

Theresa never let go of Beth's hand while they walked to the grandparents' home, it was as if she were keeping Beth safe as they continued on the narrow winding streets. As they walked closer, Beth saw Samuel outside pruning his bushes in front of his home. He wore bright red Bermuda pants, a white button-down shirt, beige sandals and an old, worn straw hat, to keep the hot sun off his head.

"Good Morning, Miss Beth. I'm glad you came," Samuel said, as he looked and smiled at her.

She in turn smiled, and then continued along the stepping stones leading up to the pale blue cottage. The roof and the window trims were white, and the Wilkerson's cottage appeared a little bigger than the one she was staying in. Theresa's friends stayed outside and continued to jump rope, while Theresa brought Beth in to greet her grandmother. Once in, Beth found herself in a large open area, with the living room in front of her and to the left dining area with a large oak table that could seat ten people. Throw rugs were scattered throughout the rooms. The walls were a yellow pastel color with oak trim, and ceiling fans hung in all three areas. Sand-colored ceramic tiles made up the flooring throughout. Lastly, she noticed a large archway/ bar with stools as she looked into the kitchen, which had the same cabinets and countertops as Beth's cottage.

The doorway leading from the dining area to the kitchen was arched also, and there Beth could see TT cooking breakfast.

TT turned with a smile, "I'm glad you decided to come. My granddaughter would never have taken no for an answer."

"Strange, she said the same about you." Beth said, responding with a smile.

Beth thanked TT for inviting her as she put the plates on the table. Theresa, having left Beth's side after leading her into the house, rushed back in the front door to see if breakfast was ready.

"Theresa would you ask your grandfather and friends to wash up and come to eat. Thank you, sweetheart," said TT, as she brought food to the table.

Once everyone was seated, TT asked them to take each other's hands and bow their heads to pray. Beth had little to say during the meal, which consisted of bacon, eggs and biscuits and hot English tea, a meal that would be the same as in Kentucky, other than the tea being served. In Kentucky, coffee was the most popular beverage for the mornings.

Afterwards with the dishes and table cleaned, Samuel went back out to work in the yard, Theresa and her friends went next door to play inside. TT fixed some more hot tea for Beth and herself, and then went to the back yard overlooking the island. But on the way out, TT poured a little of rum in her tea (TT did like a little rum now and then). Outside, both women sat at the table under a large umbrella. The Wilkerson's cottage sat on a slope, panoramic views of St. George. Beth became lost in it' beauty for just a second.

"You slept well last night," TT stated, seeming very certain.

"I did sleep well. But you already knew that, didn't you?" Beth asked with a smirk, being a little condescending.

TT took a sip of the English tea and then sighed. Slowly putting her cup down, she responded to Beth, "Yes, child I knew. There is very little that happens on this island that I don't know. I have a very strong connection with the spiritual world,"

"So you have had conversations with this spirit?" Beth questioned.

"Let us call him by his true name, Thomas. That is his name and yes, he visits often." TT replied with a nod, looking out at the view and sipping more tea. She wanted Beth to realize that this spirit once had a body and soul and lived in this world.

"Okay, Thomas. Samuel told me he is a strong spirit. What does he mean by that?" Beth asked.

With TT looking straight at Beth, she replied, "He is a powerful spirit, my child. He is able to bring you through the spiritual portal. That is how you arrived here, in Bermuda. You slept well last night because of Thomas. His energy surrounds you, he wants nothing more than tranquility for you. He was in the room last night watching over you, sitting in the chair in the corner. He will not harm you,"

Beth took hold of her cup of tea with trembling hands. Taking a sip, she asked, "How could I have not heard him?"

"You were in a deep sleep," TT replied, and continued answering questions while Beth held her forehead, looking down.

"How does Theresa know him?" Beth asked.

"Theresa and her brother, Roti, stay with us at times. Both of their parents are nurses at King Edward V11 Memorial and work long hours. While staying here, I'm sure she has seen him or heard us talking. Samuel will acknowledge his presence, but leaves us to speak alone," TT said.

"Has he spoken of me?" Beth asked.

"Oh yes child, a lot," TT replied, reaching to pat her hand.

"But why me?" Beth said, with a soft but puzzled voice, glancing back up at TT.

"Give it time. He wants to take this slowly. He will talk to you and it could even be tonight." TT said.

Tears begin to flow from Beth's eyes as TT held her hand. "You may not believe me now, but the truth will be told, child," TT said.

Beth stayed and talk more with TT, and then Samuel came to sit with them. For awhile, Beth was relaxing and at times found herself with a smile on her face. She was asked to have lunch with them and to join them for a short walk afterwards. After the walk, Samuel took Beth back to the house on the scooter.

"It will be okay, Miss Beth," Samuel said as he walked her up to the cottage door. She turned back with a smile as he pulled off down the road. When she reached for the doorknob, she hesitated as a feeling swept over her. She had a strong urge to go to the ocean. Beth turned around and walked toward Tobacco Bay. There were just very few people there. She looked out to the massive body of water and became spellbound with the salty smells of the ocean along with the sounds of the seagulls screeching above her. She watched the waves crashing against the pink sandy beach. She could see the sheer clouds coating the evening sky while the birds chirped in the bushes behind her. Beth sat down on the beach, digging her feet in and feeling the crunching of the sand between her toes. She pulled her knees up to her chest and wrapped her arms around her legs, thinking of her family. She wished she could pick up a phone and call Michael but Beth felt that Thomas would intervene. She closed her eyes for just a minute when she begins to hear a whispering voice.

"Beth, I'm here," Thomas said, who stood very close-by.

Startled, she opens her eyes quickly but was not surprised as she felt that his presence right behind her. But she was afraid to move and had noticed people were leaving the beach.

"It is time to go back to the cottage." Thomas said. Beth had her head down, while trying to find words to respond to him.

In a voice just above a whisper, Beth said, "I don't even know what to say. My life is completely upside down. I miss my husband, my family, and I want to go home."

She now could feel what she thought was his coat brushing up against her back caused by the ocean breeze. She began to see and hear his boots move through the sand. Then he stood right beside her with his duster still brushing up against her body. Still afraid to look up, she would glance over to see Thomas' boots and duster. She also noticed a missing button from the bottom of the duster. Was this the button she found under the Canadian Hemlocks in her backyard? While still looking out toward to the ocean, he spoke to her again.

"I'm sorry, but this is how it has to be. Take my hand, Beth, please."

With hesitation, Beth closed her tear-filled eyes, and then raised her right arm to feel a man's hand take hold. Both then vanished.

CHAPTER 6

LOUISVILLE,KENTUCKY: AFTER SITTING IN THE garage for hours, Michael realized he had to move and try to stay busy. He prayed to God what the spirit told him was true, that Beth would be back in a few days. He also felt the spirit's presence throughout the day he knew he was being watched, but why? He had noticed that their sons, Nick and Zach, had been trying to call their mother on her cell phone, which Michael had with him at all times. *What am I to tell them, that their mother was kidnapped by an spirit?* Who the hell will believe it? Beth's place of work also called asking about where she was. It was out of character for her not to call. Michael told her supervisor that she was very ill.

Later that evening, Michael received a call from Nick asking "Where is Mom?" He knew he had to stay strong in talking to his son.

"She has just been very busy, Nick. I'm sure she will get back with you as soon as she can. I'll tell her you called, okay?" Michael said, trying to convince Nick that his mother was fine. But Nick felt otherwise he could tell by his dad's voice, things were not okay. Nick decided to wait a few days before facing his dad and getting to the truth. Michael continued to work around the house and wait.

St George,Bermuda: Beth suddenly found herself back in the cottage's upstairs bedroom, with Thomas still holding her hand. She jerked her hand from his, then turned to walk into the bathroom closing the door behind her. Once in, Beth leaned against the door and began to tremble and cry, frightened of not knowing what could be ahead for her. When he heard the shower being turned on, Thomas walked over to the chair, removed his hat and coat, and sat to wait for Beth to come back out. After an hour of waiting, Thomas saw the bathroom door slowly opening with Beth emerging, wearing a lavender long nightgown, she held her right hand over her eyes. She could still feel his strong energy in the room. Not wanting to see the black shadow of Thomas, Beth peeked through her fingers. Then she rushed over to the bed pulling the canopy cover closed. She suddenly heard his voice,

"I'd like to talk to you Beth,"

Startled at hearing his voice, Beth responded with a sigh, "Okay."

Beth pushed herself back up against the pillows in the bed, and then pulled her legs up to her chest with her arms wrapped around them, her way of feeling protected.

"I've been told you're a spirit," Beth said, trying to find words to start a conversation with this spirit, while her insides trembled.

"I was told that you brought me here through a spiritual portal," Beth said, as she continued to talk.

"There are portals that spirits can go through and I am able to bring you with me," Thomas said. A normal man's voice, no longer a whisper, rang out, confident and strong.

"How old were you when you died?" Beth asked, trying to find the strength to continue in this conversation.

"I was 38 years old," Thomas replied.

"That is very young. What happened?" Beth asked, wanting to learn more about this spirit.

"I was shot in the chest while tending to my horses," Thomas revealed, not wanting to tell a lot of the details until asked.

She straightened her legs out. She felt a little more relaxed and comfortable, as long as she did not have to look at him.

"Do you know who shot you and why?" Beth asked.

"There were three men who came into my barn. I was coming out of one of the stalls, when I saw them. Before I could say anything, one of them pulled a rifle from his side and shot me. I died instantly," Thomas said.

Beth didn't know what to say, other than, "I am so sorry."

Thomas, wanting to change the subject, asked, "Are you hungry?"

"Yes." Beth said. Her grumbling stomach told her it was time to eat.

"There is a plate on the table. I've tried to keep it simple," Thomas told her.

Beth slowly pulled back the canopy cover, then walked over to the table and sat down without saying a word. Lifting the cover from the plate, she found a shrimp salad and crackers. A glass of ice tea sat to the side. As Beth began to eat, with a soft voice, she thanked Thomas for the meal.

After eating, she grew very sleepy. After covering the empty plate, she walked over to the four- poster bed, still not looking at Thomas and then climbed in.

"Goodnight, Beth," Thomas said, while still sitting in the chair.

"Goodnight, Thomas." It was not long until Beth was nestled in her covers and asleep.

The next morning, the sounds of the ocean rushing onto the beach and crashing into the rocks once again met her ears, and the fragrances of the salty breeze, flowing into the bedroom where Beth slept, pleasured her. She opened her eyes, but no longer felt his energy. She sat on the side of the bed and sighed. She missed Michael, her home, her family, but she knew she had no control over her life now, Thomas had that control. Beth went to the bathroom then returned to the window. Looking out to the ocean, she said a prayer to keep herself and her family safe.

On the table was another covered plate and a cup of coffee. There was also more money and a note that read:

"Good morning, Beth," It was signed by Thomas.

She looked outside again, and then sat down to eat. Fifteen minutes into her breakfast, she heard someone calling her name from outside. Looking out the window, Beth could see Theresa, Rodi, Nori, and Erica, who were instead standing in the street in front of the cottage, calling for her to walk with them. Theresa could see Beth looking at them from the bedroom window. Beth waved to them and responded with a yes. "Give me a few minutes to get ready," Beth shouted out.

"Okay, but hurry," Theresa said. A very active and mature eleven year old, she did not believe in idle time. Soon Beth greeted them out in the front and from there, they walked down Barry Road. Theresa and her friends showed Beth stunning views of St George. They made several stops so that Beth could absorb a little bit of everything, the turquoise waters that crashed against the pink sandy shores, the seagulls screaming and flapping their wings throughout St. George. Beth was told by her little guides that this subtropical coral island in the North Atlantic sat atop a long-extinct volcano 570 miles southeast of Cape Hatteras, North Carolina, the nearest land. They walked a couple of miles around St George. Several times, they stopped to rest or eat at a restaurant, (Beth paid for the meals). At one stop, Beth found herself alone with Theresa, while her friends were looking at items in a gift shop. Theresa and Beth sat at a table to drink tea and get something to eat. Beth wanted to speak to her about Thomas.

"Theresa, have you ever spoken to Thomas?" Beth asked.

"No, but I have seen him talking to my Nana outside. Why do you ask?" Theresa says, as she continued eating her grilled cheese sandwich.

Beth replied, "Because you stated the other day that Thomas was the one that left the food in the refrigerator. You were so sure that he was the one."

Theresa answered, "I heard Thomas and Nana talking about a Beth. When my grandfather stopped you that day in front of the police station, I knew who you were.

"But how?" Beth asked, her with curiosity eyes.

Theresa responded, "Thomas talked of your dark hair, green eyes and how soft your voice was and then when I heard you speak that day, I knew this had to be Beth."

As Beth tried to take in this information, Theresa continued with more. "I knew he left the food because he cares. He's not going to leave you at the cottage with nothing to eat, Beth," Theresa stated with much conviction.

"And how do you know that he cares?" Beth said.

"Because he told my Nana that he cares about what happens to you," Theresa replied.

Trying to not look stunned, Beth held her hands together on the table and smiled. The friends returned and took Beth back to the cottage. It had been a very good morning, but Beth was still in disbelief about the information that was just revealed to her.

That night, Beth felt she had to ask Thomas if he did care about her well-being. But if he cared so much, why was he putting her and her family through all this? She was very nervous about confronting this spirit due to the fact that she had only known of him a short time and knew little about him. As the night grew longer, Beth became very tired and sleepy. It had been a long day. With her eyes beginning to close, she heard his boots walking across the bedroom toward the wingback chair. She turned slowly to look, and there she could see him removing his coat and hat, laying them on the chair. She saw a dark shadow sitting there in the wingback chair. *He knows what I am thinking,* Beth thought. She knew it was not the time to question him, so she decided to go to sleep.

CHAPTER 7

St. George, Bermuda: While TT was fixing breakfast, she heard a knock at her front door. When she opened it, she found Beth on her doorstep.

"Good morning TT. I'm sorry that I came unexpected but I need to talk to you," Beth said.

"You're always welcome here, child. I'm making breakfast, would you like to join us?" TT asked.

"I'll have some tea please. Where is everyone?" Beth asked, looking around for the rest of the family. "Could you ask Samuel to call the children? They are next door. Then, after breakfast, we'll talk," TT said. Beth knew she was not given much of a choice, and knew she needed to wait.

It was such a surreal situation for Beth as she sat with the Wilkerson family in silence, drinking her English tea and listening to the different conversations around the table. She began to truly miss her family and wanted to go home. TT looked over at Beth noticing her eyes were beginning to fill with tears. It was time to take her in the backyard and talk. TT asked the children to clear the table and wash the dishes before going outside again. Then Beth and TT exited to the backyard with their hot tea. The morning's white sunlight and azure ocean breezes would help anyone to relax, and it definitely helped Beth as both women sat down at the table.

"You know what I want to ask you," Beth said.

"Not all the time, but 90 percent of the time I can tell what people are thinking. Theresa told me of your conversation with her yesterday. My granddaughter is an old soul, who can be blunt at times. She is a lot like her grandmother. Yes, Thomas does care about your well-being," TT said.

"I don't understand," Beth replied.

"The first time we met, I told you then things happen that we cannot explain and you must be patient, child, you will know, but not 'til then," TT said, while looking at Beth.

"Last night, he sat in the chair but was not speaking to me on this matter. He knew that I had questions," Beth said.

"All of your questions will be answered, in time," TT said, as she watched her husband, Samuel, who was coming out to join the women. And the conversation and Beth's questioning, ended. She realized, with a pain in her heart again, that she must continued to wait.

While in St. George, Beth tried to stay busy with the Wilkerson family and Theresa's friends, waiting for the days when Thomas would take her home to her family again.

It had been 10 days since Thomas came into the dark and kidnapped Beth from her family. In the mornings, after waking, eating the breakfast that Thomas had left for her, she would get dressed and head out, walking toward the Wilkerson's home. There, she helped Samuel in the garden with the trimming, pulling weeds and planting, which she loved to do at her home in Kentucky. Samuel taught Beth a lot about the flowers and trees that grow in Bermuda. He told her how Bermuda was most productive in growing cedar trees, and it had remained the dominant tree species until 1946, when two scaled insects killed off 95 percent of the Bermuda's cedars. But with that said, with managed land areas, there where species that could still thrive. Samuel continued telling Beth of how Bermuda has been blessed botanically speaking with a combination of abundant sunlight, high humidity and ample rainfall, allowing many exotic species to thrive on the island.

While TT helped Theresa with baking rum cakes and making jellies to sell in King's Square, Samuel would take Beth fishing on the family's small boat called Tara. He hoped it would help her to forget about her dilemma, even if it was for a short period. At times, he would look over at Beth, and he'd see how sad she was, as she stared at the ocean. Samuel would jump in trying to cheer her up by having her hold a fishing pole and showing her how to reel in the catch for the day. He noticed at times how she smiled during their conversations, showing the dimples in her cheeks. It made him think of the times when he heard Thomas talking to TT in their backyard about how beautiful Beth was and how he loved to see her smile. Samuel knew that Thomas had deep feelings for Beth.

Much time was spent in the Wilkerson's backyard, usually after meals. Beth grew to truly care about this family. There was so much love and warmth when she was around them, that it helped ease the pain of not being with her own family. One thing Beth had learned was how gracious and warm the Bermudians were. In a short period of time, she also grew to love this place and the people. But when night began to cover the island, like a warm blanket, great apprehension again overtook her. Lying in the bed, she awaited the sound of Thomas' boots walking across the bedroom floor to the wingback chair. Most of the time, he would start the conversation and Beth would only have a few words to contribute because she could think of was home. But as they continued with this encounter of talking to one another each night, Beth became aware of the fact that she felt a little more at ease with Thomas' presence. His voice was soft and filled with gentleness. Beth knew that this spirit did truly care for her and possibly loved her. But why did he love her and how did she feel about him.

CHAPTER 8

LOUISVILLE, KENTUCKY: MICHAEL WAS WORKING HARD on the side yard of the house. It had been a tribulation for the past 14 days not knowing where Beth was and if she was truly okay. He, too, knew he had no control of the situation. While working, something compelled him to look up at the driveway and the open garage door, there, stood Beth with her right arm touching the corner of the garage. Her bright green eyes looked at Michael. She swept a hand through her shoulder-length dark hair and flashed him a gorgeous smile. She looked so serene, in a long, lime green batik dress with beige sandals. Michael was over whelmed with joy but at the same time, he was filled with concern for her well being. He quietly walked toward Beth. With gentle hands, he caressed both of her arms, as if he were touching a porcelain doll, while looking straight into her beautiful face.

"Are you okay? I have been worried sick about you. God, I love you so much, Beth," Michael said, in a voice choked with emotion, holding her close, not wanting to ever let her go again.

"I missed you too. I kept thinking I would wake up from this nightmare, but I never did. Just hold me and never let go." Beth began to hug Michael with all her strength.

After a moment in each others arms, Michael and Beth begin to release their raw emotions. Their warm and wet lips met forcefully. Their souls surrender to the urgent needs that had been bottled up within them. Continuing into the house, the bedroom became their much-desired destination. Michael looking into Beth's eyes, began to pull her dress over her head, and then removed her bra. He laid her on their bed and slowly slid her underwear off, letting it fall to the floor. Staring at him, as he stood in front of her, with passion in her eyes. Beth fought to control. But with the anticipation of what was about to happen was making her breathless. With Michael's clothes falling to the floor, he slowly began to lie on top of Beth's warm naked body tenderly kissing her breasts, her neck, and her moist lips. She squeezed his back tightly as their lovemaking became more intense, with both of their bodies trembling inside. Afterwards, Michael caressed Beth's face to make sure this was really happening. She was home and hopefully their lives could return to normal.

"Have I told you how much I love you, Beth?" Michael asked, as he continued to rub her shoulders and arms.

"I love you, too." Beth said, hoping her strange ordeal was over. She began to tell him of her experience in Bermuda with meeting the Wilkerson family and, of course, there was Thomas.

It had been six days since Beth had been back. As they tried to return into a normal life, there were days when Michael would look at Beth and tell her, "It is all past us now." He was trying to convince her and himself that this incubus was over. But Beth felt differently, she had hoped it was truly over, but as days passed, she felt that it was not. She knew that Thomas had a plan and it would be carried out.

Beth called both her sons to make excuses and to apologize for not getting back to them sooner. Zach, being busy with school and work, accepted his mom's explanation of not returning his calls, but Nick thought otherwise. It just didn't add up. He knew his mom and no matter what, she would have returned Zach's and his calls. For now, he would keep his distance, but stay close enough to where if something unusual occurred again, he would get answers. He had a gut feeling that something was about to happen.

As Mike and Beth settled back into their daily lives, little was mentioned of Thomas. Beth went back to work and Mike worked on the business. Zach and Sara were coming up from Bowling Green to stay for a few days. Beth knew she would be questioned by Sara, who was very inquisitive. That evening after they arrived and were having dinner, Beth and Sara went outside with glasses of tea to sit by the pool.

"Okay, Beth, really, where have you been? Seriously, you think for one minute I'd fall for you being too busy to return Zach's call?" Sara said, as she started with her informal interrogation.

Looking at Sara, Beth began to cry, knowing she could not hide her secret any longer.

"Oh God, it's serious, isn't it?" Sara asked, feeling guilty for possibly being too hard on Beth.

Beth, wiping her tears away, began to tell Sara what had occurred for the past several weeks. "It happened." Beth said, who was beginning to relive that night. "Minnie needed to go outside around 3 a.m., so as I came into the dining room, Ricco, who had been on the couch came into the area also and began to bark viciously along with Minnie. Standing in the corner, I could see this black silhouette of a man, the same one from outside. I could see him with the little bit of light coming through the patio doors from the light post out by the pool."

"What did you do, Beth?" Sara said, frightful of what the answer would be.

"I was frozen with fear. He walked toward me, Sara. I think I fainted, I really don't remember," Beth said. Beth sat next to Sara and stared out across the pool. "I will never forget what he looked like," Beth said. Sara squeezed her hand tightly as she continued telling of the horrible experience that Michael and she had been through. "And nothing can be done, he has total control. Did I tell you his name, it's Thomas?" Beth said, as she turned back to look at her friend.

Dumbfounded on hearing this story, Sara began to think of ways of to end this nightmare for her friend. Sara asked, "How can I help?"

"No one can help." Beth said, feeling helpless and knowing nothing could be done.

After Zach and Sara returned to Bowling Green, Beth would receive daily calls from Sara. She was very concerned about the situation, but had not mentioned anything to Zach. As the fourteenth day of being home was coming to an end, Beth began to feel uneasy. She felt Thomas' presence but said nothing, especially to Michael; after all, he was contented and happy.

One evening, a week later, as Michael and Beth sat by the pool, watching the sunset, relaxing and talking of what they had accomplished that day, Beth felt a hand on her shoulder. She swept her eyes away, hoping Michael would not see how startled she was. She then turned back to give him a smile, knowing that Thomas was there with them. Finding herself shaking in her own skin, Beth then decided to tell Michael she needed to go to the restroom.

"I'll be right back," Beth said, as she leaned over to kiss his head, but at the same time needing to compose herself.

Her instincts told her that Thomas wanted her. Once she reached the inside of garage, she began to whisper (so as not to let Michael hear her). "Please go," Beth pleaded, in a trembling voice.

The evening had now turned dark, with the sun nestled behind the hills of Kentucky. Beth walks into the kitchen, with her husband still sitting outside waiting for her. The only light shining in was the light on the tall pole from outside. She wandered over to the sink and just as she was about to turn the light on, a cold chill came over her. Beth slowly turned her head toward the dining room and there he stood, a tall black shadow; it was Thomas. She closed her eyes and once more asked him to leave. With her eyes tightly pressed closed, she could hear the unforgettable sounds of his boots moving toward her. Without any warning, Beth screamed out for Michael, who jumped and looked at the kitchen window. He ran into the house to find Thomas standing in the kitchen next to Beth. She slowly turned to look at her husband, realizing the inevitable. Beth held her right arm out toward Michael, in hopes he would grab her hand and not let go. He tried, but suddenly Beth felt Thomas taking her hand. Both Beth and Michael looked into each other's eyes, knowing what was about to happen, and then Beth and Thomas disappeared. Michael's legs became weak, he had to sit on the stool at the counter, laying his head down and praying.

St. George, Bermuda: Beth finds herself sitting in the wingback chair where Thomas normally sits. She knows she is back in Bermuda. *But why is this starting again?* She asked herself. Beth is having trouble breathing. She feels the possibility of an anxiety attack occurring. Tears begin to stream down her cheeks. Night will be coming soon and she knows Thomas will be too. Beth looks out the bedroom window that she had grown to love, and then slowly walks over to the four-poster canopy.

CHAPTER 9

St. George, Bermuda: As the hours passed, Beth had drifted off to sleep when Thomas appeared at the foot of the bed, looking at her through the linen and lace that covers the canopy. He stood there for a few minutes before walking over to the chair in the corner of the room to sit down. Not ready to answer any of her questions, Thomas had intentionally waited for Beth to fall asleep before coming back to the bedroom.

The next morning, with the bright sunlight and the ocean breeze coming through the open window, Beth slowly opened her eyes and looked at the chair that Thomas sat in. *It appears to be empty*, she thought. Sitting on the side of the bed, she noticed the covered plate, a cup of coffee and a long-stem crimson rose on the table by the window. She walked over and picked up the rose. With her eyes closed, Beth inhaled the fragrance from this beautiful flower; she knew Thomas had left it for her, as if being apologetic for having her relive this ordeal. There was not a note this time as there had been in the past. But this time, a different aura existed, a feeling unlike Beth had ever experienced; she was a little more at ease with the fact that once again she had been taken from her family and home, but why did she have these feelings? With the rose in her hand, she stood beside the window looking at the spectacular beauty of Bermuda. Suddenly Beth, who had become more sensitive to Thomas' spiritual energy, felt his presence in the room. Her doubtfulness about him still made her more than a little uneasy.

"Why, what is your purpose?" Beth said, as she stared out in to the room. "There has to be a reason for you to continue with this arrangement and I would like to know what it is." Beth asked Thomas, hoping he would answer her.

And a firm voice echoed through the room, as Thomas said, "I've told you, in time your questions will be answered." Silence reigned for a few, uneasy moments.

With a softer and more caring voice, Thomas continued, "I'm only asking for this time in Bermuda to be with you."

"Can I ask, why Bermuda?" Beth said, searching for at least one answer from him.

"Because I find it to be the most beautiful place in the world, but I must go now," Thomas replied, giving in to Beth's persistence and answering the one question.

With Beth still standing by the window, she no longer felt his energy and only quiet met her ears now. She laid the long-stem rose on the table, and then sat down to remove the metal cover over the plate. But she found her appetite lacking. Beth decided to take a warm shower. Afterwards, she dressed in a green and yellow sundress with spaghetti straps; and then she put on her beige sandals. Beth felt she needed to walk; where, to, she didn't know. But as she is closed the cottage door, Beth noticed TT walking down the road toward King's Square. She hurried to catch up with her and as she did, TT finally noticed Beth.

"Good morning, Beth. And how are you on this beautiful morning?" TT asked,, as she continued with her fast- paced walk, as if she were on a mission. At times, Beth found it difficult to keep up with her.

"And a good morning to you. You knew he would bring me back, didn't you? He is telling me he wants to spend time with me," Beth said, hoping TT would unknowingly pick up where Thomas left off with answering questions.

"So Thomas wants to spend more time with you. And how do you feel with him telling you this?" TT asked while looking straight ahead and continuing on her quest.

Beth responded, "I don't know what to think or how to feel. I just want my life back."

TT glanced at Beth, with a smile, for a second as if avoiding any questions. "You look very nice this morning."

"Thank you," Beth said, almost out of breath, walking with TT.

"We've all missed you, child. I'm glad to see you again. I'm heading to King's Square to help Samuel and Theresa sell her items. Would you like to come?" TT asked, as she hotfooted down the road.

"Yes, I would like that," Beth said, while still trying to keep up with TT.

As they entered the square, Beth could hear music. She asked TT what type of music was being played.

"It is Calypso. It originated from Trinidad and Tobago. My parents could play Calypso," TT told her. She stopped for a second to listen to the music with Beth.

"Nana!" Theresa cried out, as she ran up to TT and Beth. Her grandfather Samuel was not far behind her. Theresa had a hard time containing herself when telling how much she had sold. Both Theresa and Samuel delighted to see Beth. The four continued walking down King Street, intent on helping Theresa finish selling her items. By midmorning, TT and Beth sat outside at a little Café Latte on Water Street and were enjoying hot English tea, while Theresa and Samuel went to another shop to spend some of Theresa's earnings.

Louisville, Kentucky: Sound asleep, Michael heard his name being called in the dark. He knew the voice, it was Thomas. He rose to sit on the side of the bed. He could hear his name being called again, coming from in the hall. Michael knew that Thomas was in the house, but the dogs were not barking this time. They have come to know this entity and his presence. Michael slid on his slippers and walks down the hall. When he reached the dining area, he could see a dark figure sitting at the end of the dining room table, close to the sliding glass doors.

Michael took a deep breath and called his name, "Thomas."

In the still of the night, a voice said. "We need to talk, Michael. Could you sit down please?" Thomas continued in a sympathetic voice, "Michael, I understand that you are not happy with me taking your wife once again and know you would like to fight me for her."

As Michael pulled out the chair from the table and plopped down, he asked "Is Beth okay? Is she in Bermuda?" Michael kept his head down, because looking directly at this spirit unsettled him more than a little.

"Yes, she is okay and she is in Bermuda. Beth has spoken to you of the Wilkerson family, she is with them now," Thomas said, while looking directly at Michael.

"When will you bring her back?" Michael asked, as he raised his head to look at Thomas.

"In a few weeks," Thomas replied.

"Beth is my wife, Thomas. Our lives have been totally turned around, and I do not know if it will ever be normal again. I don't understand any of this." Then slamming his fist on the table, he demanded, with boldness and fearlessness, "I want her back tonight!"

Thomas responded in a low, very stern voice, "You will see Beth when I bring her back."

Just then, Thomas slowly rose from the chair, and then vanished. In disbelief of what had just occurred, Michael put his hands through his hair. He slid the chair back and lumbered over to the patio door, thinking possibly Thomas was outside. Michael felt a wet tongue on the back of his leg, which startled him at first until he looked down and saw Rico licking his leg. "And where have you been?" Michael asked, as both walked back to the bed. Emotionally drained from his short time with Thomas, Michael turned the light on by the bed and sat on the side for a second before climbing in and cuddled with both dogs until he fell asleep.

St. George, Bermuda: After spending time with the Wilkerson's, TT had asked Beth to have dinner with them which she declined. She wanted to be alone with her thoughts. Beth walked over to Tobacco Bay Beach, and since it was close to dinnertime, just a few people were there. She sat on the beach looking out while the ocean breeze whipped around her body. And for a moment, Beth was content. Sitting there with her legs straight out and her arms stretched out behind her, Beth closed her eyes, embracing the sounds of the ocean and smelling the fragrance from the flowers; it were as if she had surrendered to this new way of life. Then she felt his presence, a gentle touch of a hand coming up from her back to her shoulder. She slowly closed her eyes, feeling his strong energy going through her body, like tiny electrical impulses. She knew she was growing closer to Thomas. With each touch from him, Beth felt a deeper emotional attachment to him. She wondered what the connection between the two of them was.

"Beth, take my hand," Thomas said while, extending his hand to her without any hesitation this time, she took hold of it. They both then vanished.

CHAPTER 10

LOUISVILLE, KENTUCKY: WITH THE SUN shining through the bedroom blinds, Michael, who was sound asleep, heard the front doorbell ring. Both dogs began to bark, as they ran toward the door to greet whoever was on the other side. Michael slowly climbed out of bed, put on his slippers and staggered down the hall to the front door. To his surprise, it was his son, Nick.

Michael opened the front door to let him in.

"You look really bad, it must have been a rough night," Nick said, as he entered the house. Nick was determined to get the truth from his Dad of what was happening in their home and to his Mom. "I just didn't get enough sleep last night. What time is it?" Michael asked, scratching his head as he walked toward the kitchen to retrieve a glass of cola to help him wake up.

"It is around 11 o'clock. Dad, where is Mom? I've been trying to call her and I get no answer," Nick said, as he followed Michael into the kitchen. "She's just been very busy, Nick." Michael said, as he takes a sip of cola trying to wake up fully.

"Dad, we need to talk." Nick said in a stern voice, standing in front of his Dad, determined to get some answers. Michael, realizing he could not hide the secret any more, walked over to the dining room table to sit down.

"You need to sit down, Nick. What I'm about to tell you will be very hard for you to comprehend," Michael said, as he took another sip of cola, needed the caffeine to kick in. He needed to be clear-minded in order to explain this phenomenon that had occurred in his family. With his dad's comment, Nick's breathing became more labored, fearful of what he was about to be told. Nick slowly sat down across from his dad at the table, looking straight at him.

"I don't know where to start, Nick," Michael said, rubbing his forehead. He continued, "Several months ago, your Mom noticed some unusual occurrences in the house and outside by the Hemlock trees. It involved a spirit. We don't know why this has happened, but two months ago around 3:30 in the morning, it came into the house and it took your mother," Michael said, still in disbelief that it ever happened.

"Took her, where? How can something like that happen? I do not understand any of this!" Nick exclaimed, in total shock to what his dad is telling him.

"He took her to Bermuda."

Surprisingly, Nick calms down and they continued with their conversation.

Nick glanced down toward the table, regaining his composure, and then he looked straight at his Dad again, saying, "Then you have to go get her and bring her back home. While you're gone, I will work on getting this house cleansed so this spirit can never enter on this property again."

"It is not that simple, Nick," Michael said, feeling a little, defeated.

"Did Mom not tell you anything about Bermuda?" Nick said, trying to figure out how to help out with this family crisis.

"She did, she mentioned a family, the Wilkerson's who live in St. George," Michael replied, still feeling helpless.

"That's a beginning, Bermuda is a small island. You should have no problem in finding this family. You find the Wilkerson's, and you'll find Mom. You need to book a flight now. I'll help you, Dad. We'll get through this, I promise," Nick said, praying inside that this would work.

St. George, Bermuda: Beth opened her eyes while still holding on to Thomas' hand. She found that they were on a very tall, black volcanic rock, looking out to the enchanting turquoise water. Waves crashed against the black rocks.

Afraid to move, or to release his hand, Beth realized the area they stood on was not large and the wind from the ocean was so strong. Beth felt if she did let go of Thomas' hand, she would be blown off.

"Are we still in Bermuda?" Beth asked, while grasping his hand in a death hold, while gaining a perception of her surroundings.

"Yes, I love this area and wanted to show it to you," Thomas said, as he looked at Beth, knowing the time was near. He turned to look at her while she continued looking out at the ocean. She turned to look in another direction when she noticed that Thomas was staring at her. And for the first time she was able to turn to look straight into his face with compassion and desire. With each touch from Thomas, Beth's heart would beat a little faster because she was growing more at ease with him. What was she exactly feeling. Could she be feeling in love with him?

Before Beth could say anything, both of them were back at the cottage, upstairs in the bedroom. Thomas had brought them both through the portal. The window was open, letting the warm salty breeze from the ocean flow through the room, illuminated by the full moon. The white linen curtains blew with the wind. In the distance, lightning flashed from a storm out in the ocean, heading to Bermuda.

Slowly releasing his hand, Beth turned to Thomas and smiled. "I want to touch your face," Beth said, as she raised her hands and gradually reached for the black, silhouetted face of Thomas.

Without words being spoken, she caressed his high cheek-bones and then up to the side of his head.

"You have somewhat of a beard and long hair." You know, Thomas, I will find out who you are,"

Beth said, with a smile, while her hands continued touching his forehead and nose.

She felt she was in a world where only Thomas and she existed, and that their two souls were becoming one.

Time had stopped as her fingers softly continued down his nose, then down to his chin. Beth could feel his wet lips and began to rub her fingers across them.

Thomas began gently touching the side of her face, running his fingers through her hair. With Beth closing her eyes, she leaned her head into Thomas' hand. No words needed to be said for both felt the same: They both wanted this moment to last forever.

Suddenly, Thomas grabbed Beth's wrists. Thomas' reaction left her in dismay.

"I need to leave for a short period. But I promise you I will return before the storm comes on shore, "Thomas said, as he gently released her wrists.

"You're leaving?" Beth asked, with some concern: she did not want to be alone with the storm coming in. Thomas slowly faded away and Beth is now standing alone in the bedroom; she wondered what she did wrong.

After a warm shower, Beth sat down at the small table by the window, still trying to rationalize her feelings for Thomas. *What does it all mean*? She could hear the thunder and lightning growing more intense. Beth had heard the storms in Bermuda could be treacherous, and she did not want to be by herself. After eating, a huge clap of thunder caused her to run to the bed. She pulled the drawstrings to let the covered white linen fall to give her more of a false secured area in her canopy bed. She sat up with her legs to her chest and arms wrapped around them. With her heart pounding, fearful of the storm, Beth began to hear objects being tossed around outside by the wind.

When the rain started, it fell fast and hard. Her thoughts were *why hasn't Thomas returned*? Suddenly Beth heard a whispering voice; it was Thomas, "I'm here, Beth. It will be okay." With the flash of lightning coming through the window, she could see the dark shadow of Thomas standing at the foot of her bed, looking at her, as he walked toward the wingback chair; she could hear the distinct sound of his boots walking across the tile. She watched him removing what appeared to be a leather coat and hat. He then laid them across the chair, as he sat down. Beth waited, and asked Thomas, "Did I do something wrong? If so, I'm very sorry."

"You did nothing wrong," Thomas said, reassuring her. Beth felt there was no more to discuss on this matter. With the storm now pounding Bermuda, Beth was able to sleep comfortably, knowing he was only a few feet away.

Before closing her eyes, her thoughts were, *That things can change in time*, as she reflected on her journey with Thomas.

CHAPTER 11

St. George, Bermuda: Samuel came into the kitchen to get a cold glass of ice water, after helping TT in the back garden. He heard a knock and with ice water in hand, Samuel walked to the living room and opened the door.

"Yes, can I help you?" Samuel asked, as he looked at this man that he did not know.

Suddenly, behind Samuel, was the voice of TT, "Samuel, don't let Michael stand too long outside. He is our guest."

With a stunned look on his face, Samuel invited Michael in.

"You can put your backpack over there against the wall," Samuel said.

"I hope your travel was good. Would you like some hot English tea? I serve only the best," TT said, as she walked back into kitchen.

"Yes, that would be nice," Michael replied, surprised that TT knew who he was when she walked from the kitchen and sat down at the large table.

Samuel was still stunned with the fact that Michael, Beth's husband, was in their home. He decided to sit down across from him, still holding his glass of ice water.

"Beth has spoken very highly of this family and she does care very much for all of you. Thank you for being there for her," Michael said, as he sipped the tea TT brought in for him.

TT sat at the head of the table, with the two men on both sides, sipping her tea with a splash of rum.

"You knew I was coming, didn't you, and my reason behind it?" Michael asked, as he watched TT drink her tea.

"Yes, I did and I do know your reason. You know he is a very strong spirit and there could be problems," TT said, as she sat her cup of tea down on the table.

"Could someone tell me what is happening here?" Samuel asked, as he watched TT and Michael staring at each other.

"Michael is here to take Beth back to Kentucky," TT stated.

Samuel looked at Michael with a look of amazement.

"Beth is my wife and who I love very much. I have to do this. She belongs in Kentucky with me. I need to salvage what is left of our life. We have our sons, and our home," Michael said, as he explained the reasoning for his presence to Samuel and TT. But clearly not understanding what was happening himself.

"You think he will just let you take her and leave?" TT asked, trying to make Michael understand there could be consequences.

"I'll take you to her," Samuel said. He felt sorry for Michael.

"I would appreciate that, Samuel," Michael replied, happy that he would be getting help in finding Beth.

As Michael and Samuel began to leave the table, Michael stopped, looked at TT and commented, "No matter what the outcome is, I have to do this for my family."

TT stood in the front of the doorway, as Michael and Samuel slowly went down the road on the scooter towards Beth's cottage. As TT smiled and waved good-bye, she began to speak to Thomas, who stood behind her, "Will you let him take her?"

"I'm letting it play out. The time is very close now," Thomas said, as he watched with TT, as the two men went down the road.

Beth stood in the kitchen washing her coffee mug, (she loves her morning coffee more than the English tea), when she heard a scooter pull up in front of her cottage. She slowly walked to the front window to look out to see who it was. To her amazement, she saw Samuel pulling away, and then she saw Michael walking up toward the front door. Beth then opened the door and ran into Michael's arms. What seemed like eternity, they stood holding each other tightly there on the short-cobble stone path.

"How did you get here?" Beth asked, still holding on-to Michael.

"An airplane and Samuel's scooter," Michael replied with a smile.

Still holding on to Beth, Michael retrieved his backpack that had fallen to the ground when Beth ran into his arms. Beth brought Michael into the living room to sit on the couch and talk.

"Nick knows everything. We sat and had a long talk about this whole situation and what needed to be done. He told me to come here to bring you back home," Michael said, explaining to Beth the family's plan.

"How did Nick take things?" Beth asked with some concern.

"Better than me actually. Nick plans to have the house and backyard cleansed," Michael said, hoping it would make Beth feel better that this nightmare would be coming to an end.

But this was not what Beth wanted to hear. She knew she had feelings for Thomas and she did not want him to leave.

"Let me take you on a tour of this beautiful island of Bermuda," Beth said, as she rose from the couch quickly, not wanting to hear any-more about any cleansing. She had Michael follow her up into the bedroom, so she could clean up and get dressed. As they came through the door, the first thing that caught Michael's eye was the large four-poster bed. As Beth continued talking about the enchantment that the island had to offer, Michael kept focusing on the bed, not hearing a word she was saying. His mind was running wild with thoughts of what possibly could have occurred in this room. As Beth retreated to the bathroom, Michael slowly walked over to the wingback chair. Beth had told him how Thomas would sit there at night, watching over her. As he laid his backpack next to the chair, Michael found himself sitting in this notorious wingback chair. He slowly re-enacted what possible things Thomas did with his hands, moving down the arm of the chair, when suddenly Beth emerged from the bathroom. Michael looked up at his wife and smiled.

"Are you hungry? I know of a nice little café on Barry Road," Beth said.

"Why, yes I am. That would be great, let's go," Michael said, wanting to enjoy being back with his wife.

After a nice lunch of fresh fish and a salad, Beth and Michael headed to Alexandra Battery Bay, a beach covered with colorful sea glasses.

As both of them held each other's hands and walked on the beach, Beth began to tell Michael the story of the sea glass.

"I was told that the bottles, jars, pottery, and plates would be discarded from ships out in the ocean. They are washed over the sand, underwater rocks and sea-shells. As a result of this, they are broken up in small pieces and the edges become naturally smooth and polished. They look like precious gems. TT and Samuel had told me of this process of the sea glass," Beth said, as they strolled together on the beach.

While walking, Michael discovered a cobalt glass covered partially under the sand. Still holding on to Beth's hand, he retrieved the glass and raised it up to the bright sunlight.

"It is very unusual to find this type of glass," Beth said, wanting to hold on to it. Michael put the sea glass into her hand. Beth then looked at him with a smile.

"We need to head back and watch the sunset from Tobacco Bay, not far from the cottage," Beth said, as they started to walk on Barry Road again. Michael was taken aback by the beauty of Bermuda and the friendliness of its people. The bright blue skies, seagulls overhead, (which appeared they were following you on the walk), and the colorful cottages that dotted the landscape of the island made him realize what an enchanted place Bermuda was. As they reached Tobacco Bay, both Michael and Beth looked out to the huge body of the turquoise water, feeling an inner peace. Michael helped Beth find a spot to sit down on the beach. They continued watching as the sun slowly began to behind the horizon and they held each other.

CHAPTER 12

St. George,Bermuda: After several hours sitting on Tobacco Bay Beach watching a breathtaking sunset, Michael helps Beth to stand up and dust the sand from her sundress. He picks up her sandals and hands them to her. They walk up to the road and head back to the cottage. Neither one of them was thinking of the dilemma they have been in. All they could think of was their strong love they had for one another.

Once back at the cottage, they go upstairs to the bedroom. Beth went into the bathroom to take a warm shower, it had been a long day. Michael sat on the side of the bed to remove his shoes then lay down to stretch his legs out on the enormous bed, covered in white linen and lace. Michael didn't care about all the feminine décor. For the first time in a while, he felt he had captured Beth's heart again and was very contented. As he was relaxing, he could hear the shower being turned on, and he smiled.

With the warm water running down Beth's naked body, she became more relaxed. Facing the wall of the shower, she put her hands up and leans against it, letting the water soak her hair. With her eyes closed, she suddenly feels someone kissing and biting on her neck. She could feel the hands of someone slowly rubbing up her arms. She felt a strong body pinning her against the shower wall. Her inner soul ignited with a flame that could not be extinguished. She turned to face her lover, Michael. They kissed deeply and passionately with the warm water running down their naked bodies. So tightly pressed together, water could not find its way in between them. With Beth's leg bent upward against Michael's outer thigh, he took hold of her leg. Both lovers are breathing heavier and soon erupt with screams of pleasure from both of them. Still kissing passionately, Michael carries Beth to the bed, stepping over his clothes. He slowly lays her down where they continued with their love-making throughout the night. The sensuousness being intensified by the warm ocean breeze coming through the window along with the moon-light.

The next morning Beth awakened from a sound sleep with bright sun shining through. Hearing movement in the room, she looked over to see if Michael was still in the bed, he was not. With just a sheet around her, she sat on the side of the bed, watching her husband packing his bag.

"What are you doing?" Beth said, with a smile and being curious. "I'm getting things ready so we can leave soon, our flight leaves in one hour," Michael said, as if on a mission of taking his wife back to Kentucky. Beth scrambled out bed, putting on her gown.

"Michael, I'm not going back. I can't, not now."

"Can't or you won't, Beth," Michael said. He is now standing in front of his wife with a shocked look on his face.

"No, that is not it, Michael. I need to know why all this is happening. Why Thomas even came into our lives and why he keeps bringing me back here," Beth said, trying to convince her husband of her reason for staying.

"Do you love him?" Michael said, looking straight into Beth's eyes searching for the truth.

"How can you ask me that, especially after last night? I love you," Beth said, who truly did not know her own feelings for Thomas.

"I thought I had your heart again last night, but I just had part of it. I just want my wife back and our lives back," Michael said, as he began to pick up his shoulder bag.

"Please, Michael, try to understand. I'm doing this for us," Beth said. She started crying while Michael opens the bedroom door to leave.

As he walks quickly down the stairs, Beth runs after him crying, begging him to stay. He walks out the front door and enters a small cab that he had called earlier. Michael looks one more time at Beth in the door-way as the cab pulls away. Beth begins to cry uncontrollably. She slowly slides down against the door frame, into a sitting position.

With Michael leaving, Beth was more determined to find the answers and to fine them now. She stood up and ran back upstairs to clean up, dress and head to the Wilkerson's home. Beth walked fast and at times ran, with tears still flowing from her eyes. Soon she found herself at their front door. No one was around, which was unusual. The children are normally outside playing and Samuel is usually working in the yard. Without knocking, TT opens the door with a smile.

"I knew you were coming. I asked every-one to stay away for now," TT said, as she lets Beth into her home. As she walks in, Beth notices two cups filled with English hot tea at the dining room table.

"You did know," Beth said. She slowly walks over to the table but does not sit down. She turns to TT, who retrieves a bottle of rum from the kitchen before sitting down at the table. After pouring just a small amount into her cup, TT looked over to Beth, who was now standing by the counter that separated the kitchen and dining area.

"Did he tell you I was coming here?" Beth said, looking at TT for answers. "I knew you were coming here after Michael left. I'm so sorry that happened. I know you both truly love each other," TT said, while looking at Beth.

"If you know this, then you need to help us!" Beth said. She quickly walks up putting her hands on the table with force, facing TT.

Suddenly the room becomes ice cold. Beth could feel Thomas' energy in the room. With her hands still on the dining room tablet, TT begins to smile at Beth.

"I think it is time for me to leave now," TT said. She gets up from the table with a sip of her tea. Beth, watches as TT opens the front door and leaves. Beth begins to breathe heavier as she backs away from the table. She knew that Thomas was in the room. She had been alone with him many times before, but this time was different. Something was about to happen that she was not prepared for.

"Say something, please!" Beth said. She felt she was about to pass out from her heavy breathing and with all the uncertainty.

"I'm so sorry that you had to endure all of this, Beth. But it was the only way. You are correct, the time is now," Thomas said, trying to explain to Beth the reasoning for him coming into her life; he then begins to walk slowly toward her.

With her back still turned from Thomas, Beth continues listening to his explanation: "I remember the first time I saw you, in front of the church doors. It was a warm spring Sunday morning and everyone was attending church from the small community, in Louisville,Kentucky. You were standing with your family. I remember you wearing a light blue dress with your black boots. Your long dark hair was pulled back from the sides with a blue ribbon. You turned and our eyes connected. I remember your beautiful green eyes, and then you smiled at me. You were the window to my soul, Beth. I knew I was in love with you at that moment."

She could tell Thomas was coming closer toward her. She slowly turns with her eyes closed towards him. Beth was beginning to feel an inner peace. Even though they have had conversations in the past, this voice was becoming more familiar to her now. She opens her eyes slowly and with a gasp, tears begin to flow down Beth's cheeks. As she stares into the familiar eyes from the past, she now knows who Thomas is. Suddenly everything became clear. He was now standing right in front of her, a figure of a tall, large built man, wearing brown linen trousers, and a white long sleeved shirt, with brown boots. His hair is dark brown and shoulder length. He has a scruffy beard and large brown eyes with thick dark brown brows. Not only could Beth see Thomas, but she knew that he was her friend, her lover, and her husband from a past life.

Beth lays her head on Thomas' shoulders, with her arms under his and her hands on his back. Still crying and realizing who Thomas was, Beth tells him, "I have been living two different lives with one heart. How can I be in love with two different men from different worlds?"

"You had to come back, Beth, to help Michael through his journey in this life," Thomas said, as he holds her tightly.

With her head pulled back to look at him closer, Thomas began to gently wipe her tears away from her face. "I have never left you, Beth, and will continue protecting you in this life. I loved you in the past, I love you now, I will love you for eternity. But I need to take you to Michael, he feels he has lost you forever. He needs to know the truth."

Louisville, Kentucky: The dogs begin to bark as Michael comes through the front door after being dropped off by cab from the airport. He feels devastated; he feels he has lost Beth. He lays the backpack down on the living room floor and then goes to the restroom. When he came out, he felt lost with Beth not being there, so he decides to drive up to Iroquois Park and take a walk. Michael parked his car at the horse barn, and then walked on the isolated road. He decided to go to the side of the road and rest on a small bench. He sat there with his head down thinking of what he would tell his sons, and how was he to live life without Beth. He begins to hear footsteps on the road; it sounded as if it was coming toward him; but he kept his head down, it just didn't matter who it may be.

"Do you care if I sit next to you?" someone said. Michael raised his head to a familiar voice, it was Beth. She stood right in front of him with her gorgeous smile. Her eyes were still red from crying.

"Beth, how did you get here?" Michael, trying to figure out how she knew he was in the park. Beth sat down next to Michael,

"There is something I need to tell you. Remember how Thomas and TT kept talking about in time when we would know what this was all about? Well that time came and I know now." As Michael looked into Beth's eyes, she continued with her story, "I've had a past life, Michael. I once lived in the early 1800's."

"I don't understand. A past life, what do you mean?"Michael asked, but, was afraid of her answer.

With some hesitation, Beth continued, "I was married to Thomas when I died from a fever."

"What! How I am suppose to believe this!" Michael said. He had a very hard time believing in this story.

"But it is true, Michael. I was brought back to help you." Beth said, trying to convince him that this is the truth.

Putting his hand through his hair, trying to take all this in, Michael responds, "Do you love me, Beth? That is what truly matters. I can't imagine going on without your love."

"I do love you and it is going to be okay now, I know that." Without saying anything, Michael stood up looking out toward the quiet road in the park.

He turns around with his arm extended out to Beth, "Would you like to walk with me, Beth?"

"Yes, I would, very much so." Beth was pleased that possibly Michael had some understanding of all of this. She took his hand and held it tightly as both of them walked to the road.

"Does this mean that Thomas is part of our family now?" Michael said in a joking manner, still trying to figure everything out.

"Michael, he has been part of the family for a very long time now," Beth replied, just letting her husband know the facts.

At a distance behind Michael and Beth, stood Thomas; He was dressed in his long worn duster, large cowboy hat and brown boots. He watched them as they continued walking down the road. Content in what he was seeing, he slowly faded away. But he would continue to watch over Beth and never being far from her.

"When we love another person, we are on a journey through life with them. However, sometimes death separates us from our partners before the journey is over." From a Unknown Author

ABOUT THE AUTHOR

Beverly was born in Sweden, England and now lives in Louisville, Kentucky. She lives in the house where she grew up, that was by her parents since 1968. She has been a Neurodiagnostics Technician for over 35 years and loves her work. She also loves to work in her flower garden and play with her three rescue dogs. She started to write several years ago after she had experienced paranormal events that could not be explained, which lead to this story.

Printed in the United States
By Bookmasters